Behind the Lines

Behind the Lines

VERNON SCANNELL

Shoestring  Press

Typeset and Printed by Q3 Print Project Management Ltd, Loughborough, Leics (01509 213456)

Published by Shoestring Press
19 Devonshire Avenue, Beeston, Nottingham, NG9 1BS
Telephone: (0115) 925 1827
www.shoestringpress.co.uk

First published 2004
© Copyright: Vernon Scannell
ISBN: 1 904886 02 7

Shoestring Press gratefully acknowledges financial assistance from Arts Council England

To Kit Wright

Acknowledgements

Acknowledgements are due to the editors of the following journals in which a number of these poems were first published: *Acumen, Ambit, Evansville Review USA, The Formalist USA, Interpreter's House, London Magazine, Poetry Ireland, Poetry London Newsletter, Poetry Review, Poetry Scotland, Rialto, Seam, Smith's Knoll, Tears in the Fence,* and *The Yorkshire Journal.*

Contents

AUNT CLARICE DANCING THE CHARLESTON

The motorway hazy, an evening in summer,
now twilit, the pause before swooping darkness;
headlamps approaching already aglimmer
but icily pale; incessant the sizzle
of tyres on the tarmac; at a touch the car radio
awakens to flavour the gaoled air with music,
saxophone, drums, piano and trumpet.

Tear-starred gaiety of prohibition ragtime
exhumes silky images of shimmying dancers,
the men in white tuxes or blazers and flannels,
the women in beaded dresses that shimmer,
shamelessly showing their silken patellas,
and I think, for the first time in years, of Aunt Clarice,
and see her in sepia, smiling in sunshine,
on the beach at Skegness, a foxtrotting 'flapper'
who never was wed, though, whenever she visited,
she arrived each time with a different 'uncle' –
or so it now seems – and with one she called Bowen
she danced the Charleston to a portable gramophone,
both of them huge in our trembling front parlour.

As a child I could sense that she did not much like me
and guessed her distaste encompassed all children.
In her smile there was something secret, unsharing,
something disturbing, beyond definition,
that carried a whiff, now just recognisable
as faintly corrupt, ambiguously sexual.

Years flickered past with no meeting or letter
till I, middle-aged, was told she was ailing,
ancient, deranged, and perhaps needing succour.
I went to her home in a North London suburb
and pressed on the doorbell. The person who answered,
an elderly nurse or companion, invited me
into the hall where I saw, on the staircase,
the crazed old woman who had once been Aunt Clarice,
the dancer of Charleston, collector of 'uncles',
now wild and dishevelled, shrieking a litany
of loathing and fear and abusive obscenities.
Her companion then thought it best I should leave.

Now twilight surrenders to night's massive presence,
the headlamps of all the oncoming traffic
are changed from pale lenses to wild glaring goggles;
like blobs of bright acid they burn through the blackness.
I switch off the radio, but not all the music
is silenced; I still hear the silvery echoes
of trumpet and saxophone, pulse of percussion,
beneath the tyres' sibilance and soft growl of engine,
as the beams of my own lights spear through the darkness,
which yields to my entry but closes behind me
on Clarice and Bowen as they dance the Charleston
in a terrible century's doomed adolescence.

REDOLENCES

Gloucester: O, let me kiss that hand!
Lear: Let me wipe it first; it smells of mortality.
                              (King Lear. Act IV, Scene VI)

Those childhood whiffs, those pungencies
and fragrances, no longer known
except in memory,
still haunt this summer evening and they bring
related images of place and thing,
black jewels of tar on sun-stunned roads,
the creaking of a garden swing.

The garden darkens, and the scents
of honeysuckle, roses, stock,
persist. Though hidden now
from sensible cognition they remain
mysteriously present in the brain
to tease, then cunningly unlock
those little cells of zest and pain.

Sunlight, the yellow smell of hay
in Folly Lane; then counterpoint
of silage and manure;
outside the inn, the breath of various beers
from open door and windows commandeers
the air with whispers redolent
of grown-up secrets, hungers, fears.

Then other odours, not quite lost
to deft imagination's net
that trawls the populous past
for sweet and yeasty scents of hymns and bells,
the sooty reek of lachrymose farewells
as train-doors slam; though we forget,
with luck, that hand, and how it smells.

A SMALL HUNGER

Ballaghadereen the place, in County Roscommon,
A time of horse-lugged wagons, vans and carts
On cobbled streets where children, men and women
Would gasp with goggling eyes and pounding hearts
To see the sky astonished to play host
To one frail, tilted, sputtering aircraft which
Swung on blue nothingness. Here, few could boast
A motor car, and nobody was rich.

I was four years old, my brother six.
We lived on tatties, fish and soda bread,
No luxuries, like buns or sugar sticks,
Except, perhaps, on birthdays. Mother said,
'Count your blessings. Others have far less.'
True, no doubt, but life for us was grim.
The Old Man doused all sparks of happiness;
Those 'others' didn't have to live with him.

Astounding now to think that he was then
No more than thirty years of age, and yet
He'd learnt already more than older men
Would know, or wish to know, of how to get
Enjoyable excitement from the pain
Of those to whom his name was synonym
For misery. We boys had often lain
In trembling dark, afraid, and hating him.

One early summer evening, back from work,
He called to us to come to him at once.
This time no glint of menace seemed to lurk
Beneath the urgency, a circumstance
Strange enough to puzzle us. We saw
His broad excited grin; his eyes were bright
With secret glee we'd rarely seen before,
A keen, anticipatory delight.

Our fear of him, though there, was modified
By curiosity. 'Come here,' he said
'I've something for you, though I might decide
I'd rather keep it for myself instead.'
He held both hands behind his back. 'Guess what . . .
Come on! What can it be do you suppose?
It's yours if you can tell me what I've got!'
We shook our heads and whispered our 'Don't knows'.

A pause and then he grinned and said, 'All right,
I'll show it you. Now shut your eyes until
I say that you can look.' We closed them tight,
And waited in our darkness while the thrill
Of expectation almost overcame
Mistrust and apprehension. Then he spoke
And broke the silence with my brother's name.
'Take it!' he said. 'Go on! It's not a joke!'

In almost utter disbelief we stared
And saw him holding up, just out of reach,
A block of chocolate. 'Cadbury's' he declared,
'The biggest size and you can have half each.'
Its blue and silver splendour dazzled us.
We gazed, amazed, and neither of us stirred.
'You want it, don't you? Well then – no or yes.
All you've got to do is say the word.'

We stayed quite still. He said, 'Be quick before
I change my mind!' And now his grin was crazed.
My brother took the chocolate slab and tore
The shining outer wrapper off and gazed
A moment at the silveriness revealed
Before he ripped the flimsy stuff away.
We saw then what the pretty wraps concealed –
A block of wood; a dummy for display.

We heard his wild, abandoned laughter skirl
and saw the demons jumping in his eyes.
My brother did not speak, nor did he hurl
The thing away. We could not find disguise
For disappointment, though we bit back tears.
What lay beneath deceitful wrappings teased
And floated on mad laughter down the years,
The ghost of a small hunger, unappeased.

GOING HOME

The light has softened from the noon's bright clamour
to a gentler tone as the evening steals
over the fields where you walk slowly home.
Hetta, your whippet, as light as a shadow,
follows at heel, and for a long moment
all sound is suppressed, a holding of breath,
suspension of thought, an unfurnished dream
or tabula rasa; then frail as a moth-wing,
source hidden by distance, no more than a whisper,
sound drifts from the river and over the meadows,
as wispy as thistledown, unseizable froth.

But now it grows stronger, is heard as a voice,
the voice of a woman, strange yet familiar,
calling the same sound, over and over;
it could be your name, the trochee repeated
beseeching six times before it is swallowed
by silence which leaves not the ghost of an echo.
And then the far murmur of traffic returning
and, nearer, the blackbird's fluting arietta
restore you and Hetta to terra cognita.
You step out more briskly, heading for home.

For less than ten seconds, perhaps, you felt young,
not happy exactly, but visited by
a phantom of rapture: the woman's voice floating
your name on the halcyon air of the evening,
calling you back to a place never known.

A NUMINOUS EVENT

Only once in my life have I experienced
A numinous event. God spoke to me.
I do not mean this metaphorically
Or by dream or through Urim or a prophet
But that He spoke to me with a physical voice
Which issued from the mystery beyond
The dark sky and its white rash of stars
On a frosty night on Ealing Broadway.
I stood transfixed, amazed, my face raised
To feel a silvery beatitude descend.

I don't remember the exact words uttered
Nor could I honestly describe the voice
Except that I would swear that it was male.
But this I do recall with total certainty:
The tone was benevolent and reassuring.
Church bells began to roll and tremble in the skies
For it was Christmas Eve and all the pubs
Had extensions of their licences.

I think God was forgiving me for my absence
From His mass. I know that He spoke to me.
Although the words themselves are lost
Or, if not lost, are hidden in the mist
Of almost half a century. And yes,
I must confess,
I might have been at least a little pissed.

BUTTERCUPS IN STORMLIGHT

Mid-June, and after five generous days
of gently fierce, unbridled sun,
the sky is plum-skin purple, tight and dark.

The air is clenched and motionless
under the undelivered tons
of thunder, yet translucent light is calm.

It is tinted, though, with mulberry.
How the quietness scents it, here by the slow river
where elderflower and cow-parsley are delicately bright.

Wild roses wrench the heart and senses,
yet nothing is so bewitching as these
clusters of familiar buttercups.

They are remade in this veiled purple day,
luminous, so radiant, glossy, clean,
so yellow that all other yellows fade.

Bananas, custard, even daffodils
are something else less yellow than these small
and unassertive, shining buttercups

that now compel, enthrall and hold
the unborn storm enraptured, so
it neglects its business and forgets to fall.

LEGAL TENDER

'Brown's made of money!' These words puzzled me
when I first heard them at the age of seven,
spoken by my grumpy Uncle Stephen.
Like a snowman's made of snow? How could he be?

Money, to me, was clinking metal, round –
ha'pennies and pennies that could buy you sweets;
the silver coins for more expensive treats
were rarely seen and almost never owned.

Each Christmas Day, before I grew too old,
I'd find, in stocking or on Christmas tree,
a small net scarlet bag and you could see
it held a dozen coins of glittering gold.

The gold, of course, was bogus, made of thin
shining foil, and yet its gleam was more
exciting than the aspect real cash wore:
it hinted sweet delight beneath the skin.

Perhaps my Uncle's Mr. Brown was made
of dollar bills, a faceless lightweight guy.
Once, I'm told, in Borneo they'd buy
goods with human skulls, a grisly trade.

Not sinister, but every bit as strange
were feather-money in New Hebrides,
salt in Ethiopia, oxen in Greece;
all, long ago, were media of exchange.

Today, approaching the Millennium's close,
the paper and the clinking stuff is less
often used for trading, though I'd guess
more is stashed away than you'd suppose,

stored in little glittering hoards beneath
old mattresses and under creaking floors,
concealed in socks inside camphoric drawers
among old photos, hairpins and false teeth.

Although ignored, forgotten and unspent
they keep some shine, survive their savers who,
whatever they were made of, had to bow
before Time's final disembellishment.

GETTING THERE

Away from the reek and hammering glare of this
loud thoroughfare where dangers lurk like mines
that smash incautious travellers to bits
you would be wise to heed those little signs
that lead to lanes and byways where you'll find
not only relative safety but, with luck,
some calmer vistas which possess a kind
of power to kindle dreams the highways lack.

Not only in the countryside, of course,
but in the streets and alleys where you smell
sly fragrances whose dark evocatory source
lies in a time and place you once knew well
but suffered exile from; in ginnels, too,
where croodling pigeon-loft and Monday's wash
compose a statement eloquent as true;
there you can stroll, or linger if you wish.

But if you yearn to reach the great good place,
or even catch a glimpse of it one day,
you know you'll have to venture out to face
the hazards of the populous highway,
and in that fiercer light and space you must
confront the risks and strike out, or be struck,
be unafraid though vigilant, and trust
your vehicle, clear vision and pure luck.

THE JOURNEY: A DIALOGUE

What preparations did you have to make
for the journey that you chose to undertake?

Not many and quite simple: lots of plain
or lined A4, warm drinks that don't contain
soporific substances, and then,
of course, a pencil or some kind of pen –
whichever is the easier to use –
thick blinds for blotting out distracting views,
stout doors for solitude and quietness,
and any kind of comfortable dress.

Did you travel with a dragoman or friend
to offer help and guidance or extend
that welcome word of reassurance when
you might have missed the company of men?

I went alone, of course, as everyone
who's been on such a journey must have done.

And did your journey work out as you'd planned,
or was there snow where you expected sand?
To put it simply, did you lose your way,
or get waylaid, or somehow led astray
by sinuous temptations? Did you keep
steady on your course or fall asleep
when senses should have been alert and clear?
Did resolution fade, then disappear?

All of those, and none.

What do you mean?

I mean that, yes I sometimes found I'd been
led by ignis fatuus or plain
laziness down tracks to bleak terrain
that yielded nothing valuable to me.
But you must understand: there could not be
a plan or chart from which to deviate:
the senses were my compass; vade-mecum, fate.

And did you succeed? How did your journey end?

I found I was unable to contend
with all the twists and obstacles I met
on that long trek. I lost a lot of sweat
for no reward. I didn't ever find
an epiphanic goal of any kind.

What is it like, this place you tried to reach?
A glittering city? Solitary beach
with whispering wavelets fingering the sand?
A place of magic, kind of fairyland?
Primeval woods where innocent killers dwell?

I'll say it once again, so listen well:
I didn't reach it, so how am I to tell?

THE VETERAN'S ADVICE

The thing you find may not be what you seek,
which doesn't mean it will be valueless;
the best approach is cautious and oblique.

At first you should have something more or less
specific in your sights – a place of shade,
perhaps, and dear remembered loveliness,

or precious keepsake carelessly mislaid –
but once the search is underway you must
forget whatever prudent plans you've made.

Let eyes and feet go walkabout and trust
the voice that whispers softly, though you may
begin to feel you're hopelessly nonplussed.

It's always best to go the longest way
to find what otherwise you might not spot,
though what that is, or might be, who can say?

Not I, or anyone, can tell you what.
Maybe the stars could say, and maybe not.

BEHIND THE LINES

Small canvas town of bell-tents and marquees
which serve as dining-hall and wet canteen;
rough-laundered khaki shirts flap in the breeze
outside most tents, for here the men can clean
those grime-encrusted garments they have worn
for weeks in stinking dug-outs, day and night,
here where the fields are opulent with corn
and they can walk quite safely in plain sight.
Distance tames the menace of the guns;
the cries for stretcher-bearers reach the ears
only at night in sleep, where wounded sons,
unmanned, cry out for mother through their tears.
These fields are sown with poppies, not with mines;
no murderous snipers lurk behind the lines.

ii

Evening, and the street lamps palely bloom
as curtained windows flush with warmth and light,
though in one high and skylit attic room
the naked glass admits incurious night
and, looking down, reflects the smooth dark face
of polished table-top on which a white
sheet of foolscap lies. The only trace
of human presence is the teasing sight
of writing – verse, it seems – too far away
to be deciphered, and a pen left there
to be picked up perhaps another day,
unless it was abandoned in despair
when this truth struck: the poem that sings and shines
lies bound and gagged, and locked behind the lines.

QUESTIONING THE MASTER

Tell me how to do it,
please tell me all you know.
I know you know the secret
that makes the whole thing flow.

Should I do it this way,
or should I do it that?
with a bottle-opener
or a cricket-bat?

I know you are an expert,
so tell me what to do,
how to go about it:
I'd do the same for you.

I've got a shining sabre,
ballet-dancer's tights,
an old Lee Enfield rifle
with telescopic sights,

a compass and a camera,
a fountain-pen and axe,
a truncheon and harmonica,
a symphony by Bax.

I've stocked up with provisions,
scotch eggs and acid drops,
a case of Irish whiskey
and frozen mutton chops.

So how do I get started?
Close both eyes and leap?
Wriggle slowly forward,
or first lie down and sleep

and hope oneiric vision
will set me on the way,
if not the following morning,
at least some time next day?

Why don't you answer, Master.
all the things I've said?
Oh Lord! I think he's sleeping
or, more than likely, dead.

IT SHOULD BE EASIER

It should be easier after all these years
of concentrated effort, some success,
the audiences' silence, hoots or cheers,

the last infrequent, as you must confess,
but though they made rare music in your ears,
their absence never caused you real distress.

The old excitement, mix of hopes and fears,
has lost its kick, the impulse to return
for one more tussle fades as darkness nears.

And if you try again you only learn
that you have lost your early snap and speed;
perfunctory applause is all you earn

and only if you manage to succeed
in going the distance. So, no matter what
they say about experience and the need

for skills that veterans alone have got,
how it gets easier, you know that it does not.

GRAY'S ALLERGY

or *More Words Overheard in the Students' Bar*

"Missed you in The Rose and Crown today.
What happened? On the wagon?
Skint again?"

"I went to Snoopy's seminar on Gray."

"You what! Old Snoops?
You must be going insane!"

"He told me Thursday, if I didn't show
I'd get the chop."

"Silly old fart . . . what did you say
the seminar was on?"

"On Thomas Gray,
his *Elegy* and other boring crap."

"But that's all medics' garbage, isn't it?
What kind of allergy was it, anyway?
And wasn't Gray the guy who wrote
that big *Anatomy*
you hear the medics banging on about?"

"No. That was Burton, and I didn't say
his 'allergy', I said his *Elegy*.
It's famous, or it used to be.
Full of quotes, or so old Snoopy said."

"Like what?"

"Like paths of glory leading to the grave
and something else about 'unhonoured dead'.
Oh yeah – here's one that even you would know –
'far from the madding crowd'. You heard of that?"

"Some old movie, wasn't it?"

"That's right. And here's another bit . . .
I wrote it down somewhere . . . it's really sad . . .
about these old blokes buried six feet deep . . .
ah, here it is!
'Each in his narrow cell forever laid
the rude forefathers of the hamlet sleep.'"

"That it?
Can't say I get it.
Who are these four rude fathers then?
RC priests or somebody's dads?
And why's he call them rude? And while we're at it,
how come Hamlet wanders in?"

"You prat! Forefathers as in 'ancestors',
and 'rude' means – I don't know – just 'rough and ready'.
Hamlet's a village not a Shakespeare play."

"All right. No need to get all sniffy.
I'm glad I don't do lit and all that shit
about old buried buggers like your Gray."

SELDOM

is an adverb
I hardly ever use;
very rarely,
almost never.
It's not that I refuse
to choose the word;
it simply doesn't come
naturally to my tongue,
although, to tell the truth,
I rather like it.
Years ago, when young,
I must have decided
for the kind of unreason common in youth
to spike it rather than speak it.
Am I wrong to say
there is something about the word
that is a little spinsterish?
Probably I am.
Perhaps it's more York Minsterish –
the Soho pub I mean,
not the place God put a match to.
Anyway, I don't suppose
you, any more than I,
give a damn,
though what seems odd
is this:
no one I know
has been attracted or repelled
by *seldom*'s adjectival avatar.
Only the poet Spenser,
as far as I'm aware,
made use of *seld*,
a word which, like its meaning,
is indeed rare.

AMBIGUITIES

English is a tongue
rich in ambiguities:
only the other day
I heard an elderly misanthropist,
with both vehemence and acuity, say
'I hate fucking youth!'

'*Youth* must be accusative,' I thought,
'but what of *fucking*?
It could be noun or verb or adjective.'
So in my quest for slippery truth
I asked him what the object was of *hate*.
He said, 'Would you repeat that last remark?'

I attempted to explain I meant no harm
but wished, politely, to investigate
what seemed to me an odd linguistical conundrum;
at which he answered, 'Fuck off mate,'
revealing further strains of ambiguity
but leaving me entirely in the dark.

FAMOUS GUEST

Frail yet pungent, gossamer and blue,
Woven by a score of cigarettes,
The light mantilla floats above the stew
Of noise, the restless heads and busy sets
Of teeth and pleasantries. The liquor gleams
And tingling glasses rise and fall in slow
Parody of beating time which wins
As win it must, except perhaps in dreams.

But this is not a dream, the famous guest
Thinks grimly as he stands with fingers round
The warming globe of glass and feels his chest
Grow tight. Soft twangings in his temples sound
As, like a small balloon, a dark yawn swells,
Filling his throat. He swallows it and grins.

Admirers gather round him, all compelled
By sly imperatives they'll later wince
About, remembering their soft surrender,
Saying 'Your last one was magnificent,
Witty, tough, yet curiously tender . . . '
'I can't think how you manage to invent
Those characters, they're all so different . . . '
'I love the one you wrote about Stamboul . . . '
'Another drink, sir? Let me fill your glass.'
He smiles. 'No thank you. Never break my rule –
Not more than three before I dine, unless
I'm safe at home where I can look a fool
With no-one's malice fed or clean dream smeared.'

At last he turns away, still smiling.
This party is a worse grind than he'd feared.
The smoke and noise begin to scratch and sting
His eyes and ears. If only he could sit
And ease the fat fatigue his calves resent.
Yet once he'd dreamed about and yearned for this:
To be raised high, a breathing monument,
Pelted with praise and hosed with adulation;
And this was what he'd feared that he might miss,
This being pumped up taut with acclamation.

A voice jabs disrespectfully and knocks
His thoughts aside. He manages a smile.
The girl's regard is confident, and mocks
Or seems to mock, but lacks deliberate guile.
'Have you by any chance a light?' she says.
And so he flicks the spring and holds the bright
Petal to her face and sees her breath
Draw in her cheeks to shadowed hollows then
Expel the ghost of smoke. She nods her head
Just once in casual thanks. He feels his grin
Still on his mouth and knows it must look dead.

She makes a flippant comment on the guests
And with her ignorant clear eyes defines
His corpulence, the hound eyes he detests
Anew each morning in the bathroom mirror,
His weariness and chronic itch of doubt,
Then turns away and with a thoughtless gesture
The cigarette and he are both stubbed out.

SPY STORY

He awoke in a strange bed
In a strange room.
Beyond the grimed window
The street with no name
Was not one he knew
Though he had seen the same
Gaunt features in other places,
The slow and shuffling gait
Of the muffled passers-by,
The faces grey and strained;
The mongrel that sniffed and sidled,
Cocked a leg against a crate:
A stale, anonymous view.
Some of the shops were padlocked.
The windows barred.
He must not linger here
Breathing the alien air,
Smelling old scent and exile.
Stale tobacco and fear.

He descended to the street,
Head down and collar raised
And began to walk towards
The spot where he would meet
His enemy or accomplice,
Assassin or assistant.
Reprieve or last defeat.

He reached the public gardens
And sat on a bench to wait
The minutes prowled past like prisoners.
It seemed he had come too late,
Or mistaken the rendezvous;
Whatever the error, he knew
His contact was not going to show.
The day began to look older;
There was nowhere else to go.
The bickering wind grew colder
And from the darkening sky,
To rest lightly on head and shoulder,
Came the frail irresolute snow.

THE LONG CORRIDORS

They are dimly lit by small electric bulbs
concealed high on the walls. The citric light
is unvaried, no matter what the clock might say;
it could be midnight now, sunset or dawn,
or the middle of the day. The rows of closed doors
are as impassive as policeman or palace-guards;
no sound behind them of altercation or chat;
on all of the floors they are identical,
except for the numbers worn on their foreheads
like insignia on soldiers' caps. The corridors
are softly carpeted, collusive with Private Eyes
and smooth adulterers. You may hear the soft whine
of the elevator as it rises or descends,
though no one enters or leaves it, except
for a sullen or shy chambermaid who bears
clean towels for some expected guest or guests.

One day, or night, you may encounter,
soft-footing it along the silent corridor,
someone who inspects the number on each door.
You will not recognise his face, nor he yours,
but of one thing you may be sure: you will meet again,
not in a long, high-ceilinged gallery, but in a place
more intimate, behind a door which he will find,
for he's always had your number and, now, he knows your face.

EPISTOLARY MARRIAGE COUNSEL

Dear Peter,
        it was good to get your letter
and I'm glad you've found the girl you say will make
the world, and all that's in it, a far better
place to live in.
        Now, you mustn't take
offence at what I feel I have to say.
Remember I am older and I know
a bit about the games that women play.
I've seen how dew-fresh virgins undergo
amazing changes almost overnight.
A lovely face of guileless innocence
when seen at 10pm in candlelight
can show, at 8am, plain evidence
of petulance, bad temper and a lack
of real intelligence, and furthermore
a sulky whine and raucous squeak and quack
replace what seemed such tuneful tones before.
So promise me you'll come to no decision
about your latest girl, or any other,
before you've undertaken this commission:
make sure you take a long look at her mother,
for there you'll see the shape of things to come.
If, after that, you still decide to marry
I wish you well, although the prospect's glum.
So Mum's the word,
               Your friend and mentor,
                    Harry.

Dear Harry,
                many thanks for your advice
which, knowing you to be a wise old guy,
I acted on at once and Paradise
itself has been the consequence. When I,
a little apprehensively it's true,
told Angela I thought it time I met
her mother Angie smiled as if she knew
about your mother–daughter claim or threat.
Anyway, the next weekend we drove
to Sussex where her mother, Isobel,
owns a little house not far from Hove.
Now comes the hardest part of it to tell.
I did just as you said I should: I gazed
at Isobel and she gazed back at me.
The spark of love ignited, flickered, blazed,
and we were both consumed. And so, you see,
your words were wiser than you knew dear Harry.
You'll see the gorgeous creature when you meet her
as you must do very soon before we marry.
Till then I am your most devoted,
                                Peter.

A LA RECHERCHE DES MOTS PERDUS

If I could find my – what-you-m'call it –
my writing-thing,
I'd start a what's-it right away,
but here's the snag, and it's immense:
I see quite clearly what I wish to say,
to celebrate or simply re-create,
but then I am appalled
to find that what the thing is called
is hidden in a haze
impenetrably dense.
Some words that used to come
promptly and obediently to heel
conceal themselves or send
unwanted surrogates
of no relevance or usefulness at all.
For example:
those delightful pretty objects, those
thingummies that smell so pleasant with their red
and velvety soft what-you-call-'ems
would, not so long ago,
have been a perfect subject for – you know –
those little teams of words that can be sung or said.
But what am I to do
when the only way
that I am able to convey
the temper of my thought and feeling is
by using words that once obeyed my will
but now are cruelly concealing who they are
and dancing just beyond my sight and reach
like graceful thingummybobs, those girls
who wear such skimpy little covering-things?
Or what's-their-names – those lovely scented things
I spoke, or tried to speak of, earlier on:
you know – they grow in what's-its
in the open air and people pick them . . . ?

No! . . . Not winners! . . . pick with fingers . . .
Noses? . . . No! . . .
What did you say then? Roses? Yes, of course!
To think that I have quite forgotten those,
when I can effortlessly find
words more abstract and more recondite,
like – you know the one I'm thinking of . . .
Oh shit! It's lurking somewhere in my mind,
yet somehow I can't quite
get the damn thing out and into sight . . .
It means forgetfulness . . . sounds like a flower . . .
You what? . . . Oh yes, *amnesia*, that's right.

CONFITEOR

I saw the warnings in my middle years
of penalties survival would impose;
it's paying-up time now – blurred eyes and ears;
scents visit memory but not the nose;
no appetite, except for phantom fare;
this hunger for lost hungers aches and grows;
dead voices whisper on the moonlit stair.

I think I could have prophesied the lot
a quarter of a century ago,
except for this one item I could not
have guessed would shake me like a body-blow,
this need to give a full account of all
the lies and selfish cruelties I know
I have been guilty of, which now appal.

If I could find a way of balancing
the scales with memories of virtuous deeds,
I'd feel less miserable, but rummaging
through those mean treacheries and lusts and greeds
I find no selfless act of charity
or bravery shines there and intercedes,
redressing the account's disparity.

And further searchings turn up nothing more
than flimsy moral negatives to weigh
against the debit side – a dismal score
of unkicked dogs and cats, a dim display
of unbruised babies, unraped girls and boys;
so 'mea culpa' as they used to say,
who prayed that God would mend his damaged toys.

PRODROME

Something terrible is going to happen,
although the world pretends it doesn't know:
an ordinary day, the shops all open,
the usual traffic moving to and fro,
and no one looks more hunted and afraid
than he or she might look on any day.

Music can be heard from open windows,
books are being read, and even written;
lovers saunter through the woods and meadows,
faint smells of cooking drift from hidden kitchens;
swans on the lake glide secretive and slow,
and still the sense of menace seems to grow.

The night arrives like other summer nights;
the music changes tempo, or it dies.
The shops are shut, the thickening dark excites
with whispering scents you can't quite recognise.
Something terrible is going to happen,
permitting no escape or compromise.

SECOND THOUGHT

However good you are, or think you are,
remember this: there's always someone better.
The smooth guy with the paunch and big cigar
denies it, but the old man in the sweater,
with flattened nose and scars above both eyes,
will nod and grin in rueful affirmation.
You'll take his word for it if you are wise
and be prepared for honeyed adulation,
that comes in floods while you're there, at the top,
to change to sour, derisive hoots and calls
when you're knocked off your perch and forced to swap
punches with old has-beens in small halls.
This is what the young will never know
and maybe it's as well that this is so.

BEFORE NIGHT FALLS

There is much to be done
and written and said,
mistakes to be rectified,
words to be read,
before night falls.

But all that you do
spawns more to be done:
if you write to your daughter
you must write to your son;
or make telephone-calls.

Day's jubilant music
already begins
to temper its tempo;
the rich mixture thins,
the eager voice drawls.

Confession, forgiveness,
perhaps time for these:
you recall the old practices?
Down on the knees
with beads or with shawls?

Or draw heavy curtains
and make the lights blaze;
remove all distinctions
between nights and days,
though the silence appals.

However you try
you can't hope to avoid
accounting for all
you have lost or destroyed
within these four walls.

So uncurtain the windows,
and, with luck, that high song
will colour the silence
beyond right and wrong,
before night falls.

BRIEF LIFE

An Epitaph

George Gordon, Lord Byron, was one of the best;
he had movie-star looks and was always well-dressed;
a bit of a cripple, but girls didn't care;
he collected their cherries and fine pubic hair. —
A versatile player at all kinds of sport
he trained on a diet of beef-steak and port
and gambled for stakes that few could afford.
He had a short innings, but boy! how he scored!

SNOW JOKE

Some time after midnight it began,
the secretive and silent transformation
of April's variegated score to one
cold and monochrome asseveration
that winter had not yet been overcome.

Next morning's curtains parted to reveal
the street and all its furnishings become,
in their white trance, intransigently still,
each motor car a furry animal,
stunned in hibernation; nameless, dumb.

By nine 'o clock no sun to modify
this black and white account of spring's defeat;
the trees in Wharfdale Park were hung with white,
but this was not the metaphoric snow
that Alfred Edward Housman wrote about.

My dog and I walked over fields that spread
before us like white parchment; feet and paws
inscribed a timeless message with their tread.
I hailed a fellow-walker, asked his views:
'Snow joke!' he called. Or so I thought he said.

TOO LATE

An evening in late July, still light, although
the sun is being slowly dragged below
the roofs of houses in North Avenue;
these overlook a small but daedal garden;
their slates are dulled and dark, no longer golden,
but the sky remains a tranquil, innocent blue.

The old man gazes through his kitchen window
and listens to the music from his radio,
a fine performance of Strauss's *Don Juan*;
he thinks, unfocusedly, of various things,
of love and music, other summer evenings
such as this; of poetry and Bad Lord Byron.

Evenings like this, except for one great difference:
then he was young, or younger, and in consequence
each day's slow dying was a prelude to adventure,
to the infinitely possible. No longer so;
for, after the sun's cremation, he will know
only a darkness like perpetual winter.

The lingering sunlight and the lengthening shades
advise that it's too late for escapades,
too late for wild nights on the sizzling town,
too late for learning Greek, for reading those
wonderful great books; for growing wise;
too late to go a-roving as the sun goes down.

KNOCKOUT

'Counted out, he (the boxer) is counted "dead" – in symbolic mimicry of
the sport's ancient tradition in which he would very likely be dead.'
                              Joyce Carol Oates. 'On Boxing'

He didn't know what hit him. That's a fact,
though now of course he knows it was a fist,
but the knowledge is posterior to the act
and at the time did not indeed exist.

And still, to tell the truth, he doesn't know
which fist it was: it could have been a right,
thrown over his defensive jab, although
a sharp left hook's been known to fuse the light.

The roof fell in and little sparklers waved
and glittered in the dark while both feet fought
about which way to go, and legs behaved
as if to stand was what they'd not been taught.

Next, a senseless page of nothingness,
a neutral tone, not black or white or grey,
immeasurable space of timelessness,
all consciousness completely held at bay.

A little death? If so, with lively hope
of resurrection in most fighters' eyes;
although the phrase can cease to be a trope,
as when poor Johnny Owen failed to rise.

A SERIOUS BITCH

Sally is a serious bitch
   She never smiles,
but something in those butterscotch eyes
   solemnly beguiles.

The question of her parentage
   remains unsolved,
though a Staffordshire Bull Terrier
   for sure was involved.

She lies, relaxed but vigilant,
   close to my feet,
alert for her next walk or feed,
   or other treat.

I know, and Sally does not, that she
   will die one day:
this knowledge seems unfair, but to whom
   I'm damned if I can say.

MISS EMILY

Behind mute walls of secrecy
She hides from peckish eyes –
While from the ivied embassy
Her unseen agents rise.

High and heavenwards they flicker
Above the oblivious town –
Her aerial messengers ride quicker
Than bobolink or sound.

Those tuneful missives are addressed
To God – or certain creatures –
And now – a century gone at least –
They come to tease and please us.

She waits in lamplight – with her Dog –
Until outwearied night
Sneaks away – and through frail fog
Slants epiphanic light.

GOD AND THOMAS HAMILTON

What falls on the doormat each day is the far
      thunder of wars and the throes
of the horribly wounded and dying, transcribed
      into clichéd mechanical prose;
and televised scenes of the broken and blind
prove starkly what humans will do to their kind.

It is foolish to try to blame God or the stars
      for the anguish and terror we've seen
men causing each other, and then offer prayers
      that divinity should intervene;
but what of those other disasters we name
as 'from natural causes'? For these, who's to blame?

The hurricane, earthquake, the flood and the drought?
      The infanticidal disease?
If God loves his creatures, as Christians maintain,
      how can he give sanction for these?
Not only permit them, but aim from the sky
new ways for his victims to suffer and die?

I presented this question to one who might know –
      a thinker and man of the Church –
who told me the answer would not be revealed
      to those whose crude methods of search
were based on the limited reason of Man,
which would hope to discover an ethical plan.

But God, he assured me, is not of the World,
      His 'thereness' beyond time and space;
His motives and deeds as impenetrable as
      the inscrutable mystery of grace.
Like the actions, I wondered, of him who had slain
those doomed little children that day at Dunblane?

The name, Thomas Hamilton; his smallish arms
        were for culling not cuddling the young;
No one could guess, when he entered the school
        where, shortly before, they had sung
their simple sweet hymns, his revered Smith and Wesson
would be used by its owner to teach them a lesson.

CARPE DIEM

How quaint those visions of the future seem,
expressed in verse or, as more likely, prose,
whose source lies not so much in waking dream
as sour distaste for how the present flows,
or fear of new directions it might choose,
as if their authors could divert the stream.

The scenes devised do little to persuade,
like models built from kids' construction-kits,
dated within days of being made;
Utopias, or their dark opposites,
can do no more than flimsy movie-sets
to make us feel more hopeful or afraid.

Those beardless prophets Orwell, Huxley, Wells,
paddled in a future we now see
as concrete history. Our little hells
are much the same dark holes they used to be,
and Eden's gates stay locked. So seize the day,
no matter what the latest seer foretells.

INDIAN SUMMER

This day is wholly unsullied,
golden and beneficent. I sit
in my recommissioned deck-chair
by the garden path. From a cerulean sky
the sun's unwinking stare
fixes the world in stasis, warm and somnolent.
This is the weather of myth.
Not a rumour of air
stirs in the limp laburnum, or anywhere;
all is so still and soundless you could hear
the wing-beat of a moth,
except that from my open window drift
faint sounds of Strauss's *Tod und Verklärung*
and yet more faintly, now and then, is heard,
closer, underneath my hand,
dry whisper of a turning page
as I peruse, with awful delectation,
The Oxford Book of Death.

ROPE DANCE

The last dance of its kind and never again
these morning bells, their cruel carillon
counting the breathings of that young man and woman
who will not kiss, or be kissed by, anyone
ever again. Not that they kissed each other
as lovers, or chastely as sister and brother,
for they did not know one another. And, as they dance,
it's not in graceful tandem in a trance
of silvery sound and with the slinkiness
of Rogers and Astaire, but separate
in time and space, a frisky jig or foot-dance,
kicking and treading frantic air until,
with one last goodbye twitch, their feet are still.

Cocked to one side, each blind and hooded head
seems interrogative, though what might be said
is anybody's guess. Nothing perhaps.
The choreographers in robes and wigs
or starry epaulettes and smart peaked caps
swap slippery grins, though venture no slick answer.
The crowd outside is heard to sigh and murmur,
though not by either motionless rope-dancer.

CASTRATI

Morning: coffee-breath still staining the air
which carries, too, a contrapuntal sound
drifting from the radio, the strains
of Handel's opera, *Guilio Cesare*.

On Radio 3 of course. Cesto is sung
by a counter-tenor whose crystalline alto,
the presenter announced before the broadcast began,
bears little resemblance to how the old castrati sang.

How would they sound to us, those ancient high warblers –
the famous Farinelli, say? We are told
by learned musicologists their voices
were more powerful than the cool altos of today.

Yet, in imagination's auditorium,
when I try to re-create the sound, I hear
not so much power as a pitiful distress –
a high, waiting cry of inconsolable loss.

DYING LIKE FLIES

'In Chaucer's time, of course,' the speaker says,
'all human lives were cheap. Far more than wars,
the Black Death killed off countless multitudes.
People of all classes died like flies . . . '

'Like flies?' a somnolescent listener wonders,
and thinks about the fly-deaths he has seen,
remembering those dangling, film-like strips,
glossily slick with toffee-textured glue

and speckled with black and scrunched-up little thorns.
He can't mean those? Or smashed by paper clubs,
quick splat on wall or window-pane? The Plague
never dispatched its victims with one smack.

In Chaucer's time, as now, folk died like folk,
cursing their fate or praying for salvation;
dying, they knew quite well what they were doing.
The fly's way seems the better way of going.

CASUALTY

Just after 4 a.m. he is brought in.
The urgent ambulance that carried him,
and briefly startled sleeping city streets,
delivers its limp cargo and retreats.

A weary charge-nurse says, 'What happened here?'
The paramedic's mouth is skewed and grim:
'Some yobboes out for laughs had too much beer
and kicked the living daylights out of him.'

Kicked the living daylights out of him.
But now the dying nightlights flicker, dim,
before going out, and then the blinds are drawn.

Beyond drained windows birds are heard to sing
by patients as they stir and stretch and yawn.
All taste the waking day, except for him.

A KIND OF GLORY

(In memoriam: Howard Winstone 1939 – 2000)

I

A winter night, the chapel windows bright
with lemon light against the misty dark,
the little houses huddled close for warmth
and mutual protection; you, just twelve,
running down the narrow street, alone,
each breath exhales a spectral bloom, your boots
belabouring the pavement as you pound
your panting way beyond the Workmen's Hall,
past slag-heaps and the pit-gear of the mine
and onward to the hilly countryside:
you're training hard, as grown-up fighters train.

Two nights each week you work-out at the Club,
skipping, groundwork, and the heavy bag,
then, best of all, the sparring in the ring
when all the theory and the fluent moves,
the fantasies of perfect stratagems,
so sweetly economical and swift,
are acted out as sweating fact
                              You know
that you will be a champion one day;
you have to be. All of your waking thoughts
are focused on perfection of your art.

Wealth, the noisy worship of the crowd,
might come, but these are never what you crave.
Your love is for one thing itself, the pure
enactment of the perfect moves, a blend
of the aesthetic and the agonistic which,
as spectacle, is thrilling, but to do
is pastime for the Gods, a true vocation.

II

British Schoolboy Champion at your weight
in 1954; then, schooldays ended,
what waited was the factory or the pit.
You chose the factory, though you intended
staying there no longer than the time
it took to reach the statutory age
when you could leave and start the long hard climb
towards the first and necessary stage
beginning the ascent that every keen
pugilist attempts – a national title.
Your choice proved almost fatal. A machine
snatched and mangled your right hand. Three vital
fingertips snapped off. The shock and pain
were fierce, but far more cruel was the small
explosion of awareness in the brain:
that hand would never make a fist again!

And yet it did, through your determination
not to be denied, although this fist
at first was just a formal imitation
of that destructive weapon you had lost,
and though a measure of its strength returned,
you knew its imperfection permanent.
But your unquenchable ambition burned
more brightly still and it was evident
that you would not surrender. Changed by sheer will,
what seemed to be a vicious trick of fate
became a spur to even greater skill
and speed of rapier left to compensate
for loss of knock-out power in that maimed right.

You then set out to scale the towering hill.

III

Howard Winstone, dedicated fighter,
you did not look the part: too slight, too handsome.
When you, as amateur, were picked to fight
for Wales against the English someone said,
'That boy is far too frail to fight as pro.'
Your trainer, Eddie Thomas, answered him:
'He'll win tonight and when we both decide
it's time for him to turn professional
he'll be World Champion, I promise you.'
And those unlikely words, in time, came true.

IV

The Noble Art, Sweet Science, what you will,
always your vocation, now your trade,
you followed it at home in Ebbw Vale
and Aberdare, the tragic valley towns
you knew and loved so well; then far away,
in London and in Rome, your dazzling skill,
that silvery speed and sleight of feet and hands,
balletic poise and elegance, amazed
and thrilled the crowds no less than your displays
of immeasurable courage and astute
control of each bout's varying demands.
You almost always were victorious
and yet the most consummate exhibition
of your now famous fighting qualities
ended in your dubious defeat.
In 1967, and at your peak,
you fought in Cardiff, fifteen sizzling rounds
against Vicente Saldivar, the great
Mexican whose legend still resounds
wherever fighters meet to celebrate
the heroes of their sport.

That night, beneath
the pitiless candescence of the light
gushing from the lamps above the ring,
you faced the tigerish attacks of one
whose will to win was forged in hammered steel
and met each fierce assault, each hook and swing
and uppercut, with cool and stylish skill.
Your left flashed out, you feinted, sidestepped, swayed
and stabbed again. The dark roar of the crowd
was oceanic, surging in huge waves;
you heard it, not with ears but in the blood.
You foiled the Mexican's belligerence
for thirteen rounds and victory drew close,
but then he smashed through your fatigued defence
and you were on the floor. The crowd's vast voice
was briefly choked and then it was transposed
from exultation to heart-broken woe;
but then it rose again as you, too, rose
to face another onslaught and survive.

The contest ended and the referee
turned towards your corner, then he paused,
and seemed to hesitate; then suddenly
he faced about and moved to Saldivar
and raised the right hand of the Mexican
as winner of the fight. The clamorous roar
of that Welsh multitude was once again
grief-stricken but was seasoned now with rage
as your old friend and handler, Thomas, raved
with anger and frustration. But you shrugged
and crossed the ring to Saldivar and threw
one arm about his shoulders and each hugged
the other wordlessly, survivors both
of one ordeal, co-authors of a true
unwritten epic work to celebrate
pure courage, grace and skill, a kind of love.

V

A hard light, icy, in the corridors
although the air is warm enough; a mix
of smells – distant cooking, laundry scent
and something antiseptic, surgical,
obscurely menacing. White-coated men
and women, preoccupied and serious,
swish on their important business past
slow stretcher-trolleys and their human freight,
one of which is trundled by a short
and stocky grey-haired man of middle age,
his features worn and blurred with weariness,
though there is friendly humour in his eyes.
He wheels his trolley through the swinging doors
to where a male nurse helps him heave his charge
from stretcher on to bed. The porter nods
and says goodnight to nurse and patient, then
he wheels his empty trolley out of sight.
The nurse says to the patient, 'Do you know
who's just now brought you back from being X-rayed?'
'That little porter? No, I've no idea.'
'That was Howard Winstone.'
'Howard who?'
'Winstone the boxer, Champion of the World,
just brought you back and put you into bed.'
'I've never heard of him,' the patient said.

VI

Howard Winstone, Prince among
the finest warriors we have known,
skilful, brave, you stood alone;
but now the final bell has rung.

And all around is heard the sound
of jagged musics and the air
trembles with a chill despair:
nobility lies under ground.

56

Juggernauts of flesh and bone
lumber round our tarnished rings
launching ponderous prods and swings,
no tune, but tedious monotone.

These clumsy antics are, in part,
gross parodies of what, with skill,
you rang your changes on until
the thing became a work of art.

Old men, it's true, in every age
have claimed the world will never see
again the likes of who might be
the leading player on their stage.

But you were truly nonpareil:
the other tiny giants, Wilde
and 'Peerless' Driscoll both beguiled
and thrilled the crowds, and yet their tale

for sheer enthralment can't quite rise
to that intensity of pitch
of your life's variegated, rich
poem delighting heart and eyes;

an epic narrative that rose
at times in breathless lyric flight,
though ending with the dying light
in bleak and elegiac prose.

And though the splendour of your story
has not been, as it should be, told
and carved in characters of gold,
it still bequeaths a kind of glory.

So let the valleys ring with praise
and gratitude for their brave son
whose every battle, lost or won,
enriched the fabric of our days.

Howard Winstone, Prince among
the finest warriors we have known,
skilful, brave, you stood alone;
but now the final bell has rung.

A SMALL EPICEDIUM

I am in mourning, though you wouldn't know
from anything I wear that this is so.
It is not possible for me to share
the hurt, nor make it easier to bear
by formalising it in ancient rites
with choristers and priests and acolytes,
for what I mourn is not a long-loved friend
or close relation's lamentable end
but something I alone am broken by,
who didn't think it would ever die:
I mean of course – I wonder if you've guessed –
the tiny talent that I once possessed.

PLANNING THE OCCASION

Music and just one poem, not too long,
but something that will pierce right to the bone
and linger in the head. It would be wrong,
I think, to choose a work that's too well-known
or anything too slick and up-to-date:
something by Herbert, or a Shakespeare song,
should strike a note to chime and resonate.

The music, though, is harder still to choose:
it must be something easy on the ear,
yet serious stuff. Not New Orleans blues,
that trails a haze of sex and smoke and beer,
nor anything austere, like late Baroque;
and yet the smooth and richly sensuous ooze
of Suk or Gluck might come across as schlock.

That's not the thing we want, so I must find
a work so lovely it will make them weep
a salt monsoon; don't think I'm being unkind,
for grief of that sort isn't very deep
and holds some spice of pleasure; so I swear
they'll have a ball. That's why I'm not resigned
to not being there, or anywhere at all.

OTHER BOOKS FROM SHOESTRING PRESS

POEMS Manolis Anagnostakis. Translated into English by Philip Ramp. A wide-ranging selection from a poet who is generally regarded as one of Greece's most important living poets and who in 1985 won the Greek State Prize for Poetry.
ISBN 1 899549 19 6   £8.95

HALF WAY TO MADRID: POEMS Nadine Brummer *Poetry Book Society Recommendation.*
ISBN 1 899549 70 6   £7.50

BROXTOWE BOY: A MEMOIR Derrick Buttress. ISBN 1 899549 98 6   £8.95

TESTIMONIES: NEW AND SELECTED POEMS Philip Callow. With Introduction by Stanley Middleton. A generous selection which brings together work from all periods of the career of this acclaimed novelist, poet and biographer. ISBN 1 899549 44 7   £8.95

Shoestring Press also publish Philip Callow's novel, BLACK RAINBOW.
ISBN 1 899549 33 1   £6.99

TARO FAIR Ian Caws. ISBN 1 899549 80 3   £7.50

THE WEIGHT OF COWS Mandy Coe. ISBN 1 899549 97 8   £7.95

INSIDE OUTSIDE: NEW AND SELECTED POEMS Barry Cole. "A fine poet ... the real thing." *Stand.* ISBN 1 899549 11 0   £6.95

GHOSTS ARE PEOPLE TOO Barry Cole. ISBN 1 899549 93 5   £6.00

SELECTED POEMS Tassos Denegris. Translated into English by Philip Ramp. A generous selection of the work of a Greek poet with an international reputation.
ISBN 1 899549 45 9   £6.95

THE NEW GIRLS Sue Dymoke. ISBN 1 904886 00 0   £7.95

COLLECTED POEMS Ian Fletcher. With Introduction by Peter Porter. Fletcher's work is that of "a virtuoso", as Porter remarks, a poet in love with "the voluptuousness of language" who is also a master technician. ISBN 1 899549 22 6   £8.95

LAUGHTER FROM THE HIVE Kate Foley. ISBN 1 904886 01 9   £7.95

THE HOME KEY John Greening. ISBN 1 899549 92 7   £8.95

KAVITA TF Griffin. ISBN 1 899549 85 4   £6.50

LONG SHADOWS: POEMS 1957–2000 JC Hall. ISBN 1 899549 26 9   £8.95

A PLACE APART Stuart Henson. ISBN 1 899549 95 1   £7.95

CRAEFT: POEMS FROM THE ANGLO-SAXON Translated and with Introduction and notes by Graham Holderness. *Poetry Book Society Recommendation.*
ISBN 1 899549 67 6   £7.50

ODES Andreas Kalvos. Translated into English by George Dandoulakis. The first English version of the work of a poet who is in some respects the equal of his contemporary, Greece's national poet, Solomos. ISBN 1 899549 21 8   £9.95

OMM SETY John Greening. ISBN 1 899549 51 X   £5.95

FIRST DOG Nikos Kavvadias. Translated into English by Simon Darragh
ISBN 1 899549 73 0   £7.95

A COLD SPELL Angela Leighton.*Other Poetry*. ISBN 1 899549 40 4   £6.95

WISING UP, DRESSING DOWN: POEMS Edward Mackinnon.
ISBN 1 899549 66 8   £6.95

ELSEWHERE Michael Murphy. ISBN 1 899549 87 0   £7.95

TOUCHING DOWN IN UTOPIA: POEMS Hubert Moore
ISBN 1 899549 68 4   £6.95 Second Printing

MORRIS PAPERS: POEMS Arnold Rattenbury. Includes 5 colour illustrations of Morris's wallpaper designs. *Poetry Nation Review*. ISBN 1 899549 03 X   £4.95

MAKING SENSE Nigel Pickard. ISBN 1 899549 94 3   £6.00

THE ISLANDERS: POEMS Andrew Sant. ISBN 1 899549 72 2   £7.50

MEDAL FOR MALAYA: a novel David Tipton. ISBN 1899549 75 7   £7.95

PARADISE OF EXILES: a novel David Tipton. ISBN 1899549 34 X   £6.99

STONELAND HARVEST: NEW AND SELECTED POEMS Dimitris Tsaloumas. This generous selection brings together poems from all periods of Tsaloumas's life and makes available for the first time to a UK readership the work of this major Greek-Australian poet. ISBN 1 8995549 35 8   £8.00

AT THE EDGE OF LIGHT Lynne Wycherley. ISBN 1 899549 89 7   £7.95

COLLECTED POEMS Spyros L. Vrettos. ISBN 1 899549 46 3   £8.00

TAKE FIVE: poems by Ann Atkinson, Michael Bartholomew-Biggs, Malcolm Carson, George Parfitt, and Deborah Tyler-Bennett.   ISBN 1 899549 90 0   £7.95

For full catalogue write to:
Shoestring Press
19 Devonshire Avenue
Beeston, Nottingham, NG9 1BS UK
or visit us on www.shoestringpress.co.uk